Astitva Prakashan

Bilaspur, Chhattisgarh 495001
First Published by Astitva Prakashan 2021
Copyright © Soudia Parveen 2021
All Rights Reserved.
ISBN: 978-93-91219-04-8
Price: Rs.199/-

WORLD OF MY WORDS

Soudia Parveen

Acknowledgement

————◆————

I belong from an Islamic family, that doesn't mean that I have grown up in an Orthodox family.

Everything I do today is what I chose for myself and not what my society expected or approved for me.

The biggest supporter in my life is my parents.

I have encountered situation where my friends were bound to put on a "hijab" (a religious veil worn by Muslim women in the presence of any male outside of their immediate family, which usually covers the hair, head and chest), but I never experienced such dominance from my family and it was absolutely my choice of putting a "Hijab" and live without hesitation.

The reason behind my choice is my unique identity and proving some people wrong in the society who has a misconception about girls covering their head and having no caliber to do something worthy.

I am here to prove that a girl can have the potentiality to explore even if she covers herself and chooses to work.

My parents always supported me through every decisions I took for myself. "

All credit goes to my father (Mr. Sk Ishaque Ali) and my Mother (Mrs. Hena khatun).

Thank you,

- Regards
SOUDIA PARVEEN

About The Book

It took me one long year to write this book,

I hope one hour of your precious time will not be so long enough to dedicate to my book.

This Book is a Versatile collection of poems, shayaris, articles about women exploitation, women empowerment, love, motivation, inspiration, life events and many more, which aims at reaching out to the society in a different format to catch their attention and not their boredom.

To make it to your taste,

The book is written in precise poetries and quotations and in a very short format, for you to go through it within an hour or a week most probably.

This is my dream book and my parent's dream which is accomplished today.

I hope my people will bring a success to my hardwork!

Thank you,

Regards

Soudia Parveen.

About the Author

Soudia Parveen is a Psychology student from West Bengal, kolkata and is a passionate writer.

Most of her writings belong to women exploitation and daily happenings. She mostly writes on those women who are not safe in this pace of life. She is a highly motivated person with an aim to achieve one goal at a time. She says that she has never been proud of having a caliber as writing such poems on the most debatable issue all across the world that is "the state of women!"

Therefore she says that she could feel the extreme out of the daily happenings which doesn't make some of the women, in some society safe and secure.

The lines she puts in her poems and quotes are random thoughts which comes to her mind.

Sometimes it comes in free verse and mostly in rhyming form.

As a writer, she just wants to explore and never put an end to her writing life.

She accepts that she is not perfect but she never quits in life. She keeps on trying till she

achieves what she wants to.

Lastly, she leaves a deep message to all that:

"Life cannot be understood until

You ride the waves

Float like a boat,

And swim underwater!"

MY JOURNEY

Soudia Parveen says, "My life was full of threats, till the day, I made relation with certain people with certain mutual acerbity.

During my school days, I was a very average student and my parents were humiliated with every initiative they took to educate me in a reputed institution.

My mother faced various obstructions from my family for not letting me achieve my dreams and every time I had my examinations, I could encounter hindrances on my way.

I didn't like socializing much before because of these reasons!

But when I slowly started encountering the harsh realities of life, I was able to come out of the feelings of disdain and contempt.

I try my best to do limited work with uttermost perfection and I don't let myself to get engaged with things which I know I can mess up with!

So yes, last but not the least, I had like to mention this that no matter what, I keep on trying new things and I don't hope for the best outcome anymore but yes I believe one failure means thousands of achievements.

The most beautiful thing I have achieved is to take stand for myself and I do not hesitate anymore because I feel, I have that much sharpness and directness in my speech which helps me out in clearing or putting forth my thoughts!

My childhood was not so happening but my present is rocking!

Today I do everything with a determination to get a neutral result!

Being good among five people and being better than someone is more than enough for me!

I am not perfect I know. That is why I have made a mindset to live with small units but qualitative!

I'd like to end up saying:

"DON'T DREAM MORE BUT DREAM BIG"

I am Soudia and this is my story!

I write about them,
And they are unaware of it.
They tell me their story,
And I make it my content.
They share their feelings,
I keep on jotting down the situation which I can imagine
through their gesture!
I keep on putting emphasis on their story!
And they think,
I am a writer with multiple experiences!
They are the people who give me a new story to pen
down!
They are the one who forces me to frame a poem out of a
decade journey.

I am a writer,
My contents are different always!
Everyone thinks it to be my life's experience,
But no!
I live in their world through their words and gestures!
Because,
I believe a writer has the potentiality to experience
through someone's gesture itself!

~ SOUDIA PARVEEN

Table Of Content

YES, I AM A GIRL!

Yes, I am a girl!
And a precious pearl.

Don't measure my breast,
And put me on test!

I dont roam with my friend,
Cause I know it ain't my trend!

I am that wine which you had taste,
But I'm fine cause I know it ain't a waste!

Don't touch me for a gain,
Stop giving me such pain
Someday all your deeds will go in a vain,
You can't really touch me again!

Don't buy my body, it ain't a brand!
You know someday, this body will take a stand!

I want to be a cloud,
Which teaches not to be aloud!
'Cause it doesn't speak through lines,
All is expressed through it's outlines!

I surely hope,
Someday I'll cope!

∼ **Soudia Parveen** ∼

With a spreaded wing,
I'll fly away from this hatred ring!
And that day, will be "MY DAY",
When no one but I will say!
About the pain,
they gave me then
And I'll end up singing a song,
To prove the patriarchy wrong!

YES YOU CAN DO!

Just raise your voice,
They'll surely praise your choice!

Just be the judge,
With the personal grudge!

To the men out there,
Flyin' high in the air!

Don't have to be shy,
Cause time passes by!

Just spread your voice,
As much as you can!

Cause you know it babe,
They won't judge you back!

Yes you can do!
Yes you can do!
At the end of the day,
Everyone will remember you!

~ Soudia Parveen ~

MINE!

---◆---

I'll make you mine,
Through every possible hurdles!

I'll treat you soberly,
In every possible means!

I'll stitch your broken memories,
If it is remained a nightmare to you!

I'll conceal your mistakes,
From the judgemental society!

I'll efface your scars,
As time passes by!

I'll fight with your negative mind,
To uphold your positive heart!

No matter what,
I'll make you mine!
And I'll treat you
like "mine" eternally!

CHEER UP BAE!

———◆———

Oh! my dear bae,
Stop thinking about me all day!
I am constant,
I'll stay with you!
My love is everlasting,
I'll be there with you!

But what about the time which waits for none?
Just silently work hard until the rise of the sun!

It's still your precious time,
run behind every success!
It's not a time to rest,
it ain't your school's recess!

Don't worry my dear,
There's really nothing to fear!

You might have failed yesterday,
You might not get what you want today!
But tomorrow with loads of success,
it will only be "YOUR" day!

People will persistently humiliate you,
'Cause they have no other works to do!

But you still know the fact!

~ **Soudia Parveen** ~

How much calibre you do possess,
Simply just ignore their speech and
walk to the path of success!

Always do remember how intelligent you are!
There is a right time for you,
which is not really far!

Always remember dear,
People will speak nonsense 'bout you
Standing upright behind you!
And never in front of you!

Cause they know it well,
No matter how much they tell!

You will surely show them one day,
That under any circumstance
You won't ever go astray!

OH! MY DEAR SOCIETY JUST SHOW UPON US SOME PITY!

Don't judge me by my past,
Don't judge me by my cast.

Dont divide me into a race,
By judging my entire face.

It tortures me with pain,
Cause my society is insane.

My dress defines my culture,
Am not a useless sculpture.

I know I don't have a beautiful face,
But definitely not your showcase.

I seriously can't help it out,
Even though I desperately shout.

I am a human like you, wanting for some space,
Running rigorously in this long race.

In such a patriarchal society,
I still search for some matriarchal propriety!

Oh! my dear society,
Just show upon us some pity!

~ Soudia Parveen ~

SORRY FOR HAVING A VAGINA!

———◆———

Dear body,
I am sorry for having a vagina.

My vagina is on sell,
Where the vendor is the consumer itself!

Although I possess two holes down,
I have no access to it!

My breasts are meant to get smacked.
The mamilla are meant to be drawn into the mouth,
The haunches are specialized flesh, to get spanked!

Above all,
The curves around my belly
is to be held tightly,
By some strange hands
I also have the idea of getting my muscles and spine
broken as soon as my seal is ruptured!

Oh! I wish I had no openings in the vulva,
I would probably be safe just
as my father and my brother!

Dear body,
I am sorry for having a vagina!

THAT PITCH BLACK NIGHT!

———◆———

Flashback encountered as she slept,
    It started with that pitch Black night!
    Her body unwinded inside the ill-lit room,
'She heard the whisper again'

"The whisper", which was not unusual to hear,
Was by the man who slept right beside her again!
He certainly puffed against her ears
And firmly grabbed her breasts,
She gasped in pain and tried escaping all over again!

The very moment she remembered the first time she did
bleed,
Thereafter she wished of being paralyzed,
Alas! Forcefully it was for her,
to sense the deepest pain!

Sudden realization headed towards her mind,
That those similar hands are still scrolling all over her
body through out!

 "It's the right time to break the awful days"
        — Her soul whispered to her ears

Right beside the bed was kept a Filleting knife,
She firmly grabbed it in her hands
And finally stabbed it on her STEPFATHER'S back!

She penetrated the knife more with his yell with uttermost pain.
This time she smiled after ages of dreadful nights.
 * (After the flashback) *

> As she opened her eyes,
> She was proud of her bravery
> Of breaking an end to her strive!

Hence, the pain she was given was not more than her stepfather's ridiculous death!

CHEERFUL PERSON WITH A DEAD SOUL!

Gloomy weather, Sad emotions!
Happy faces but blank mind!

I am screaming as much as I can,
Alas! No one can hear!

Loud voice within but silence throughout!
Rain outside is washing away,
All the happiness of yesterday!

Where am I?
Oh Yes!
Drowning with the struggle to
achieve self actualization!
Yes of course, I am here,
in the midst of hell and heaven!

Just because I am breathing,
doesn't mean I am alive!
Just because I am smiling,
doesn't mean I am happy!

I dont want to be anyone's sunshine,
Instead I want to be someone's
rain where they can dance!
I am not completely pessimistic,

~ **Soudia Parveen** ~

Nor I am completely an optimistic personality!

I smile when I want to,
And never ever did I fake it!

I am sorry to my soul for being a mess!
And to pressurize it with
loads of works and responsibilities
even though it didn't want to perform!

Yesterday I felt that I am just loosing everyone!
Other day, it made me realize that I gained a truth!

Even if my society thinks, I am not worthy!
It's just because of the gloomy weather,
Otherwise I am a motivated
and a cheerful person with a dead soul!

WHAT IS A FEMALE'S ROLE?

A Responsible lady for my family,
Immature in front of my beloved!

A stern woman to those nasty strangers,
An entertainer in front of my friends!

A jolly young lady in front of my professors,
A careless woman from outside in stressful moments!

Smiling to the fullest in worst times,
Always being a motivator for
the ones who had lost hopes.
Balancing life with job and household works,
but still living with full energy!

Back pain is not an issue anymore,
because my mind approves me to turn
a mountain into a road!

After these,
You ask
What is a female's role?

~ **Soudia Parveen** ~

BUCKLE UP BOYS!

————————◆————————

Dear Boys,
Before you get old and regret then!
Do something worthy,
either for your parents or your society!

Firstly,
Instead of investing your hard-earned cash
on your beloved, Save it for your future!
You never know, Where your destiny turns,
So if you are in love, better work on getting each other for
the lifetime with achievements meant for a healthy life!

If love is all about material gifts
then trust me you must move on,
A better version of your ex is waiting for you!

Dear boys,
if you havn't travel yet on your first job's salary and had
spent that money into some useless stuff then you are
going wrong!

Boys!
Set up your own business and if you are into a job then
burn the midnight oil to get a higher post in a reputed
company!

And if you are still a high school "cool buddy"

Then put on your formals,
Leave behind your torn jeans and funky shirts!
It's time for "great achievement's level 1"
which means your college life!

So boys, there are a hell lot of things
to do besides knitting your love life!
It's good to be in a relationship but it's not
good to put your life into a morose zone!

Buckle up,
My dear boys!

~ **Soudia Parveen** ~

LIFE UNDER THE ROOF!

————◆————

Life is too short,
To achieve thousands of dreams.
And the "inner me" is too weak to
encounter the present situation with courage.

The four walls around are admiring me throughout,
The hanging window sash are spying from behind!
The clothes beyond my wardrobe
glances at me out of pity!
As if, all of it are willing to,
shower mercy to the "infirm me"!

Am I being an attention seeker?
Well, my "inner me" is too busy to be sulky,
That it can act enthusiastic
to the mates under the same roof!
My fellow bed is playing the role of a cactus
to my haunches, which pricks me
from behind whenever I try to relax on it!
My mind is busy sketching the future I'll
encounter!

My heart is engaged in dealing with the emotions,
My pillows are flirting with me to sleep over it,
every minute I gaze on them!

Thus, the only living thing bothered about me

are my so called "parents",
Who out of nowhere comes to me,
surveying on my anticipation every few hours!

How more can life be worst under a roof?

~ **Soudia Parveen** ~

NIGHT BEFORE THE EXAM!

Tick tock of the clock,
My recitation went aloud!

That night, the moon shone so bright,
Putting me in a state of fright!

"Knock knock!" (Mother shouted....)
            "Get in! "(whispered my cold lips.....)

Mommy stood upright offering me, a glass of milk!
My hands which shivered,
couldn't get a hold of it,
I ended up splitting it, all over the quilt!

She stroked my hair and calmed me down,
With utmost nervousness I fiddled around!

What was really bothering me so much?
Yeah! the very next day was my examination.
I was told to gain good marks
to earn a good reputation,
But as usual my books and I had no cooperation!

Slowly I recovered from being helpless!
Cause I got aware of the marks, I was going to get,
Which would surely make both of my eyes wet!

MY EVERYDAY KISS!

Every morning I wake up,
All I do is to pick you up
Keepin' the edge on my finger tips,
I kiss you with my cold lips!

On the time of gloomy winter,
When I hold you in between my finger
You give me a warmth sensation,
Removing previous night's frustration!

Your hot sizzlin' aroma,
Is like the plants of cinchona!
Which helps me remove my grief,
And give the most relief!

Every eve when I put on "like a virgin" by Madonna,
I end up dancin' "Like a burgeon"
in the midst of flora and fauna!

I kiss you every morning,
I kiss you when 'am crying!
I kiss you every evening,
I kiss you when 'am bleeding!

When I get tired of this kind of life,
I remember to kiss you my co- wife!

I will keep on kissin' you till 'am breathing,
I will keep on tasting you till the day 'am leaving!

You are not a human as they see,
But my "crystal cup of tea"

INDIVIDUAL'S ROLE!

———◆———

Your heart is an apparatus,
Through which you speak!

If your heart showers negativities,
You tend to be a defeatist!
And certainly project a,
gloom-ridden character on others!

If people judge's you on account of
your personality and behavior,
Then remember!
Somehow it is you,
who made such a comfortable
expression on others,
That now they have started
pointing out negativities in you!

Similarly, people who makes verdict on you,
Sometimes project their own behavior on you!

Everything has a link,
Everything is interrelated with each other!

In order to balance things
Try and avoid judging others,
And make yourself flawless!

Sort things out by yourself first,
Then depend on other's perspective!

DEAR FRIEND!

---◆---

Dear friend,
A decade together,
We have seen the most of life!
I am occupied in the darkness alone
My soul assures me :-
"Here comes the one to lighten up
the Inferiorities to superiority "

Guess who?
Ya' the one,
Who brushes my hair when 'am painted with "henna"
The one who feeds me with her hand,
When 'am injured!

Ain't my backbone, but my confidence!
Ain't a moron, but over possessive!

Nah! She ain't dramatic
She's a bit over protective,
Than the rest of the backbiters!

Since a decade!
She'd been acting as my crown,
Never letting me have, a chance to
Put my head down!
Ain't among those nasty ones,
Considerably the better one!

Hey,
Wait!
Who?
Finding it cryptic?

Let's reveal then!
Of course,
My constant, my main
My friend who stands by me on my worst!

Hey lady,
Will you like cracking
jokes even in the crypt?
Will you be mine forever?
Yay! Of course
Untill we both turn Spectre?

THE FUTURE BONG BRIDE!

I believe,
The sun will be upright shining
And that day I'll be draped in a red saree,
Traditionally pinned all over!

I don't know how that morning would seem,
But I know the fresh Garland of flowers
around my hair bun will mesmerize
the people around me with it's beautiful smell!

My presence on that morning will be
different and attractive to the people all around,
My hands and feet will be painted
with the red dye "Alta",
And my forehead will be decorated
with a floral design "Alpana"
I will be up on bed,
resting my legs like those on sidesaddle!
Around me will be those beautiful ladies,
Who will admire me and call me as their own sister and
would console that they consider me to be an essential
part in the family!

I believe,
I would be shy to have an eye contact with my spouse!
But meanwhile, we will admire each other and promise to
support each one through our thick and thin!

Even though, one is not in many people's good books, but
we will assure each other
that we will trust one another and be their backbone!

The day will be bright,
But the responsibilities from then
will double up for sure!
Yes, that day I will be someone's wife,
someone's Sister-in-law,
and someone's daughter-in-law!

I believe,
The day will start beautifully,
And I will be blessed with the
strength to take responsibilities eternally
in a new family with unusual faces!

THE INSTANT FEELING!

—————◆—————

When I speak to you
My Heartbeat gets fast,
Pulse rate increases!

I bite my lips more than I usually do,
I keep on staring at your eyes
I keep on observing the way you smile!
I don't know Who you actually are to me,
But I know, I can't afford to loose you!

You are someone very close to my heart.
May be I am breathing today because of you,
Maybe I am in desperate need of you!
Whenever am extremely happy or sad!

Babe trust me,
You are the first one to whom
I am able to share both the negative
and the positive chapters of my life!
I smile when I am alone
but with you I am able to laugh!
I have started loving things
more intricately than before!

Your existence rather than your love
matters more than anything else.

Last but not the least,
I love you!

~ **Soudia Parveen** ~

BAE!

I was just thirteen, when I met with him,
When I used a cell, without a sim!

That time I wanted him like the heart needs a beat!
And I was sure of the fact,
his heart will definitely give me a seat!

Love at first sight was so much strong,
Never had I thought will last so long!

It's hard to find a perfect guy,
But I got that one under the blue sky!

Whenever I fear of loosing him, I cry
But thereafter I pray,
He shouldn't leave before I die!

You will also fall for him, if u hear him speak!
What more to say?
He's so much unique!

Yeah! May be my "bae" is a piece of antique!

Yeah! It has been so many years now,
I had spent with him!
Who really knows?
I may further bear children of his!

I am ready to carry the burden of his heart forever,
I wish to marry him,
and own that precious treasure!

Doesn't matter if my heart turns a stone,
I'll still be there for him as a backbone!

He is not only my heart
But an integral part!

I love him now !
I loved him then !
I'll keep loving him,
till the day I won't breathe again!

~ **Soudia Parveen** ~

YOU!

————◆————

You aren't a wifi,
but I still find a connection!

You aren't a person with all perfection,
But I still don't have any objection!

You aren't a thief,
but have stolen my heart!

Just telling you in brief,
You are my oxygen sweetheart!

You ain't there with me 24/7,
But one minute of conversation,
Makes me feel like I'm in heaven!

You are so much humble and kind,
You are the only person in my mind!

I dream of you frequently,
Which comes to me everyday ceaselessly!

When everyday, I dream of marrying you,
I hope all my dreams will someday come true!

You are a cool person with great charms,
All I need is to wrap you forever in my arms!

LOVE NEVER DIES!

———◆———

Before I sleep,
I'd like to inform you
That the touch of your
cold lips on mine
Under the blanket
will be the best part
of our short journey!

A cup of coffee in a gloomy winter,
Was still better with you!

Long conversation throughout the night,
Cheered up the "morose me"

Pressing each other's body in a snowy evening,
And feeling the cold breath will be missed!

The fights on some silly reasons
was meanwhile the key to
pour affectionate love on each other!

Putting jazz and dancing on the garden
Was a better version of our mental workout!

I am at a loss for words,
Everything is towards an end
But I remember you saying,
"Love never dies"

~ **Soudia Parveen** ~

EROS!

Dear,
I know at times I behave really very bad!

But at the end of the day,
your ignorance makes me very sad!

May be I am broken into pieces,
and scattered all over ur heart!

But u won't really care to show,
even if I try very hard!

I want to hug you tight,
After a real long fight!

Just stay with me dear,
Am gonna stay only for a while!

TOXIC LOVE!

Oh gosh!
He is so perfect,
I had mistakenly thought!

And I took him to be a worthy man,
which he was really not!
And I loved him dearly
But towards the end,
Things became so toxic!

We no longer had the passion, respect, trust and the
abundant love we once shared!

~ **Soudia Parveen** ~

NIGHT AFTER FIGHT!

————◆————

The fight was just a reason,
For us to meet again!
He entered and clasped me as usual,
Yeah! I could feel the grip in his arms this time,
"The longingness to sense every
texture of my body considerably"

He whispered softly to my left ear:
"I'd like to make extreme love tonight"
As he murmured this,
I felt his goosebumps on my skin!

Pushing me towards the couch,
He nuzzled over my navel!
The slightest tickle made me
embrace his muscular body!

When his beard poked while the interaction of our lips,
I got aware of the hungriness
he experienced since ages!

Pressing the skin around my waist,
He clutched over my bosom!

The night that followed,
Just smelled and vibed like those of lavenders!

LOCKDOWN DIARY : DAY 38!

The sky is pouring rain,
But we can't dance along with it!
Yes! being within four walls is a tough job,
but we stand united once again to Fight something big!

We know today we watched
the raindrops through our window,
Who knows?
May be, tomorrow we'll dance in it!

Yes, we all know that today we are
locked in our house and connecting
to our dear ones only through video calls!

But tomorrow,
I believe that everyone will get the chance
to hug their dear and near ones tightly and say:
"This lockdown taught me one thing,
That how much valuable you are when I don't feel your
existence!"

A bright tomorrow is waiting for everyone!

~ **Soudia Parveen** ~

CATASTROPHE!

A stormy evening!
Delicately curved with the thunderstorms
and dark clouds.
Firmly Knocked my window shelter,
Destroyed the window Shields!

A sudden noise cracked my doors and
Within milliseconds the nearby house broke apart!

Dear God,
I wanna know?
Will we face no more peace?
Shall we wait patiently still?
'Bout to be a year, but no relief
from the major outbreak!
But welcoming more disasters
with a smile unwillingly,

I was waiting for God's response
With uttermost patience within,
But meanwhile,
I received a news from my pal that
her native land has encountered a "boom" sound,
'Bout which no one is aware of what it can be?

Labours have no wants for money,
but the necessities hit them hard!

They need no shelter but flatbreads for twice a day!
Economy goes down, it becomes a chaos all over!
But hunger pangs and poverty did not matter to be in a
headline's disclosure!

~ Soudia Parveen ~

CHILDREN'S SEASONAL DIARY!

Sunday nights,
On Sparkling spring
With spring rolls and drinks,
They play jigsaw and build blocks!

Monday Fun day,
On Summer vacation
Ice cream in one hand,
They roll on beach land!

Tuesday evenings,
When Monsoon beckons
Mommy prepares hot bowl of noodles while,
They dance on the lawn along with the raindrops!

Wednesday sunsets,
On dark stormy lanes
With hot fried french fries,
They listen about grandma's childhood days!

Thursday afternoon,
Autumn diaries
With milk and cookies
They open their books and studies!

Friday morning,
Bright chilly winter

Packs hot sandwiches
For school's recess
They bunk their classes and plays chess!

Saturday sunrise,
Having Heavy snowfall
Drinking hot espresso!
They run out of house
To make snow house,
Out of ice!

SHAYERI KI DUNIYA

Likhne ka shawk mera dus saal purana hai,
Kalam haath pe pakra zaroor thaa
Ye sochkar ki ek din kaviyetri kehlaungi!
Kavitaa o se shuruaat zaroor ki,
Magar lakshya shayeri pe palat gayi!
Jo likha kavitaaye maine,
Aaj tak logo ne kiya prashansaa!
Par aakarshit kiya jo logo ko,
Wo meri kavitaaye nahi
Meri likhi huyi kuch dil ki alfaaz hai!
Kuch ashiqui main mili bewafayi,
Kuch logo ne kiya mera ye haal!
Ki aaj jab bhi, fursat se likhne beth ti hu
Kaviyetri nahi shayara kehlati hu!
Jo baat dimaag se likhti hu,
Wo kavitaa ban jaati hai!
Bethu agar likhne dil se,
Toh mehfil jama deti hu!

~SOUDIA PARVEEN

JO SATH THE, UNHE AB YAAD NAHI KARTE
HOJAYE KISISE ISHQ, TOH IZHAAR NAHI
KARTE!
KISISE AB HUM DIL KI BAAT NAHI KARTE,
JISSEY KARTE THE WO DIL TODHKE, BAATO KA
GALAT MUDDA BANATE GAYE!
FIR BHI HUM UNKI FARIYAAD NAHI KARTE!
AAJ KOI KARDE PYAAR KI IZHAR,
MUJHE MAJBOORAN KARNA HOTA HAI
INKAAR!
AUR LOG SAMAJHTE HAI KI MUJHME BHARI
HAI AHANKAAR!
NAHI SAMJHANA AB KISIKO,
NA KARNA HAI AB BAYAAN ISS DARD KAA!
HAR JAGAH AB CHHAYI HAI AAFAT,
KYUNKI AB HAMARI RUH ME BUS GAYI HAIN
NAFRAT!

~ SOUDIA PARVEEN

JO KARU THODA KHULKE BAAT
TOH MUJHE MULAYAM MIJAAZ KA NAAM DETE
HO
HAS LIYA KABHI, TOH "KATILANA HAI YE
ADAAYE" BOLA KARTE HO!
JO NAZAR MILI KOI ANYA PURUSH SE,
TOH BEMATLAB, CHARITRAHINN KA DARJA
DETE HO!
JO RUTH GAYI TOH MANANE NAHI AATE HO
BHAVNATMAK DHAMKIYA DEKAR,
KHUD CHAIN KI NEEND SOYA KARTE HO!
TUMHARI HARKATO KI WAJAH SE JAB DURR
CHALI GAYI MAIN,
KUCH AUR NA KEH SAKE TOH ZAALIMA
BOLAA KARTE HO
KAB TAK MUJHE YU BEWAFA KEHLAAOGE
GALTIYAA KHUD BHI TOH KARTE HO,
FIR BHI AKELA SHIKAAR MUJHE BANAYA
KARTE HO!
BADA HI GAJAB KA VAAD HAI AAPKA,
PYAAR KI MAANG HUMSE KARKAR
IZZAT DENE KI BHI SAMARTHYA NAHI RAKHTE
HO!
PYAAR EK TARFA THODI HAI,
JO UMMEDEIN HUMSE HI
LAGAYA KARTE HO!

~ SOUDIA PARVEEN

MAIN AKELE UNKI POORI KAINAAT HU,
AISE POORE DUNIYA KE SAMNE UNHONE
ELAAN KIYAA THAA!
JIS KHUDA SE MUJHE WO MANGA KARTA
THAA,
AAJ BESHAQ WO MERI MAUT KI MAANG
KARTA HAI!
JISNE KABHI APNE DIL PAR HAME JAGAH DIYA
THA,
SUNA HAI KISI AUR SHAKS SE PYAAR KI IZHAR
KARNE JA RAHA HAI!
KHAIR,
KHUSHI ISS BAT KA HAI KI
HUMSE JUDAA HOKAR BHI WO KHUSH HAI!

~ SOUDIA PARVEEN

TU UDAS HUA JO,
MAIN KAINAT SE TERI KHUSHIYA WAPAS
MANGUNGI!
TU RUTH GYA JO,
MAIN KAANCH KI DHAR PE APNI ZINDAGI KO
BIKHAAR KE RAKH DUNGI!
TUJHE KOI AUR DUKH POHCHADE,
TOH SAMAJH JANA USKI QAYAMAT AAJAYEGI
US DIN!
JO CHHOR TU GAYA MUJHE,
PURI DHARTI KO MITAA DUNGI!

~ SOUDIA PARVEEN

TUMNE SIRF MERE JISM KO NAHI,
MERE ROOH KO CHHUA THAA!
MANA KI TUM CHALE GAYE CHHORKE,
PAR SATH REHNE KA WADA TUMNE BHI KIYA
THAA!

~ SOUDIA PARVEEN

WO KAINAAT HAI,
TOH MAIN TERI TAQAT!
WO JAAN HAI,
TOH MAIN GUROOR HU TERI!
WO SAANJH HAI,
TOH MAIN JALTI DIYA!
WO SAGAR HAI,
TOH MAIN BARASTI VARSHA!
WO ZINDAGI HAI,
TOH MAIN VISHVA HU TERI!

~ SOUDIA PARVEEN

TUJHE,
MERA SUKH BARDASH NHI THAA
MERE CHEHRE KI MUSKAN PASAND NHII THII
NAFRAT THI TUJHE JIS MUSKAN SE
CHODH GYA TU JIS WAJAH KE LIYE,
AAJ DEKHO NA!
LOG MARTE HAI MERE ISS MUSKAAN KO EK
DAFA DEKHNE KE LIYE!

~ SOUDIA PARVEEN

ISHQ NIBHAANA JAANTA HI NAHI,
TOH BEWAJAH HUMARE DIL MAIN
DAKHIL HONA HI MAT!
TUJHE DIL TODNAA HI HAI,
TOH KABHI LAGANA BHI MAT!
SATH CHHORNAA HI HAI
TOH RISHTA JODHNAA BHI MAT!
AGAR TU KEHTA HAI KI TUJHE AAGE KAA
PATA NAHI,
TOH FIR HUMSE WAASTA RAKHNAA HI MAT!

~ SOUDIA PARVEEN

SARD KI SHAAM HAI,
BAAHON MAIN LAPETE KAMBAL HAI
PAAS RAKHI EK CUP ADRAK KI CHAAYE HAI,
AUR HATH MAIN EK KHAT HAI
WO KHAT JO LIKHA THAA UNHONE,
MUJHE PICHLE SARD KI MAHINE MAIN!
USS SARDI KI SHAAM KI BAAT HAI YEAH,
JAB KHAYALO MAIN, WO RAHA KARTE THE!
PAR ISS SARD MAIN KOI NAHI BASTA MERE
KHAYALO MAIN!
NAA HAI KOI AISA SHAKS JISSEY DIL MAIN
LIYE GHUMTE HAI,
AAJ MUJHE APNE JAZBAT,
APNE AAP SE PYAAR HAI!
DEKHONA JANAB,
AAJ KHUDKE SATH KHULKE JEE RAHE HAI!

~ SOUDIA PARVEEN

TU MERA MEHBOOB NAHI HAI,
NAAH HI TU MERA PREMI HAI!
TU MERE DIL KE KITAAB KI EK AISI ADHYAY
HAI
JISKI KHUSHI PE MUJHE JASHN MANANA HAI
AUR JISKE RUTHNE PE MUJHE USKA SAHARA
BANNA HAI!
MERE DOST MERE JIGAR!
MUJHE TERI KAMZORI NAHI,
TERI TAQAT BANNA HAI!
PURE KITAAB MAIN DUKH WALE KISSE BHI
HOTE HAI, AUR HOTE KHUSHIYO KI BOHOT
SARI MAATRAAYE,
TU EK BOHOT ZAROORI PANNA HAI MERE
ZINDAGI KE KITAAB MAIN!
KYA PATA SHAYAD TU HI AAKHRI PARICHHED
HAI!

~ SOUDIA PARVEEN

TERI MUSKAAN MUJHE ISS QADAR GHAYAL
KAR JAATI HAI KI MERI DHADKANE BHI MUJHE
PUCHNE LAGTI HAI :- "MAIN THODI DER KE
LIYE RUK JAUN KYAA?"
MAIN PUCHTI KYUN?
TOH WO KEHTI "AISI KEEMTI MUSKAAN HAR
KISIKO NASIB THODI HOTI HAI?"
WAHI MERI SANSEIN BOL UTHTI HAI :-" BURA
NAA MANO TOH EK BAAAT KAHU?"
MAIN PUCHTI KYA?
TOH WO KEHTI :-" KI ISS SHAKS KE PYAR MAIN
ISS QADAR GIR CHUKI HU MAIN, KI AB TOH
TERE JISM MAIN REHKE BHI SANSEIN INKE
NAAM KI LIYA KARTI HOON!"
MAIN HAIRAANI SE JAB ISS JUNOON PAR
AITBAR KARNA CHAHTI,
TAB HI MERE ANKHON SE EK AWAZ AATI :-
"IJAZAT HO AAPKI TOH EK FARMAISH MAIN
BHI HOON RAKHTI!"
MAIN BECHAINI MAIN PUCHTI "KAHO KYA
KHWAISH HAI AAPKI?"
TOH WO KEHTI :- "MUJHE IJAZAT DO KYUNKI
AISI ANMOL SI ISHWAR KI SHRISTI KO DEKH,
YE PALKE KHUD BA KHUD HAI JHUKTI"

~ SOUDIA PARVEEN

MUJHSE AANKH CHURAATE HO,
APNA PYAAR CHUPATE HO!
SAHELIYO SE SUNAA KI,
CHUPKE SE MERI TASVEER KHINCHTE HO!
MERE LIYE SUBHE KI TAZI FOOL BHEJTE HO,
AUR KHAT MAIN MERI MITRA KI NAAM LIKHTE
HO!
SUNA HAI MERE LIYE MASJID JAATE HO,
NAMAZ MAIN MUJHE MAANGTE HO!
MOHALLE MAIN MERI GEET GAATE HO,
AUR KOSHISH PYAAR KO GUPT RAKHNE KI
KARTE HO!
ITNA HI PYAAR KARTE HO,
TOH SAMNE AAKE KYU NAHI KEHTE HO!
AAKHIR KYU MUJHSE AANKH CHURAATE HO,
KYU APNA PYAAR CHHUPATE HO?

~ SOUDIA PARVEEN

WO JO HUMARI CHUP CHUP KE,
TASVEEREIN KHENCHAA KARTE THE!
AAJ KHUSHNASEEBI SE,
UNKI TASVEER MERE RISHTE KE LIYE AAYI
HAI!

~ SOUDIA PARVEEN

SHAADI TOH UNHI SE KARUNGI,
JINHONE AAJ TAK MERE GHARWALO
KE KHILAF EK SHABD NAA KAHA HO,
JAB MERE GHARWALO NE
UNKI MOHABBAT PE UNGLI UTHAYAA
AUR UNHONE BIN KOI SHIKAYAT
MUSALSAL MOHABBAT NIBHAYA!
HAAN MAAN LIYA WO SABSE
KAAMIL SHAKHS NAHI,
MAGAR AURON SE MUKHTALIF ZAROOR HAI!

~ SOUDIA PARVEEN

ISHQ ITNI MAZBOOT HONI CHAHIYE
KI DUNIYA NAA BHI RAZI HO TOH SHAADI
KARNE KE LIYE DONO KI RAZAMANDI AAKHRI
HO!
AUR DUNIYA CHAAHE JITNI BHI DARAARE
LAAYE,
BICHADHNE KE LIYE DONO HI RAAZI NAA HO!

~ SOUDIA PARVEEN

WO LADHTE HAI,
APNAAPAN JATANE KE LIYE
BEETE HUYE KAL KI EHSAAN NAHI!
WAQT DETE HAI,
MOHABBAT SAMAJH KAR
ZIMMEDAARI NAHI!
HAQ JATATE HAI WO
BIWI SAMJH KAR
RAKHAIL NAHI!
WO SHAWHAR HAI MERE,
MUKHALIF NAHI!

~ SOUDIA PARVEEN

TUM JAISA KOI AUR HAI TOH
USS BHEED MAI,
MAIN TUM HI KO CHUNUNGI!
TUM NAA CHAAH SAKO,
TOH BHI MAIN TUMHE TOOTKAR CHAAHUNGI!
KHYALAT ALAG HO TOH KHUDKO BADALNE
KE LIYE TAYYAR HO JAUNGI,
TUMHE TUMHARII TARIKE SE JEENE DENE KA
AZADI DEDUNGI!
KHUDA MERE AAGE HAZAR MOTIYAA ZAROOR
BICHHAA CHUKE HAI,
MAGAR MERA DIL TUM JAISE HEERE KE LIYE
HI DHADAKNE KA ZID LIYE BETHA HAI!

~ SOUDIA PARVEEN

AYINAA KEH RAHI HAI,
UNKI ANKHON MAIN KHUSHI,
DARD KI CHEEKHE CHILLAA RAHI HAI!

~ SOUDIA PARVEEN

KUCH RISHTEY TEER JAISI HOTI HAI,
CHUBHKE REH JAAYE TOH HAR PAL DARD
DETI HAI!
AUR NIKAAL FEKNE PAR MAUT SI TAKLIF
ZARUR DETI HAI,
MAGAR ZINDAGI BHAR KI DARD SE REHAAYI
DE JAATI HAI!

~ SOUDIA PARVEEN

CHAAHNE WALO KI KAMI
TOH NAHI HAI,
MAGAR SUKHE REGISTAAN KI TARAH
IS DIL MAIN MERE,
BUS AB CHAHAT PAANE KI JAZBA
KHATAM HOGAYI HAI!

~ SOUDIA PARVEEN

AE ZINDAGI, TU ITNI BHI KHUDGARZ NAA BAN,
KAHI MERI DOLI KE JAGAH
MERI MAYYAT NA UTH JAAYE!

~ SOUDIA PARVEEN

BINA SIKHE, MOHABBAT NIBHANE CHALI THII,
ANJANE MAIN KISIKAA DIL TODH AAYI!
KHAMOSHIYO KO THUKRAKE,
SAHARA KHAMIYO KO LAGATI GAYI!
ISHQ KA PATA LIYE NIKLI THII,
MAGAR NAFRAT KI GALI PE AAKE JAA
POHACHI!
MOHABBAT KI YE SAMANDAR ME,
MAIN FIRSE AAJ HAAR KE LAUTI!

~ SOUDIA PARVEEN

LOG KEHTE HAI :-
"ISHQ MAIN THOKAR KHAAKE
ZINDAGI SE MOHABBAT KARNI CHAHIYE"
MAGAR MERE YAAR,
"SACCHI ISHQ KI THOKAR BARDASH KARKE
TOH DEKHO
ZINDAGI SE MULAQAT BHI KAR NAHI PAAOGE,
MOHABBAT TOH FIR BHI BOHOT DURR KI BAAT
HAI"

~ SOUDIA PARVEEN

LOG KEHTE HAI :-
"ISHQ KARKE ISHQ KO MAT CHHUPAO
DUNIYA KO DIKHAO, MOHABBAT JATAO"
MERE YAAR,
"MOHABBAT SE AZIZ YAARI DEKH, HAR ZUBAN
MAIN ITNE CHARCHE HAI,
SOCHO MOHABBAT KI MUNKASHIF KARNE SE
HAR JAGAH MAIN KITNE MEHFIL JAMENGE,
MEHFIL MAIN KUCH HONGE JO HASAD
KARENGE
AUR KUCH TAUSEEF KARTE PAAYE JAAYENGE "

~ SOUDIA PARVEEN

CHAND TAARON KA TODH LAANA
MERE BUS MAIN NAHI,
MAGAR TERE MUSKAAN KO
BARAKARAR RAKHNE KA
ZIMMEDAARI BESHAK NIBHAUNGI!

~ SOUDIA PARVEEN

AAJ FIR EK SUBHA MERE NASEEB HUYI HAI,
CHEHAKTE HUYE PAKSHIYON KI JHUND LAGI
HAI
SURAJ KI PEHLI KIRAN MERE
ANGAN MAIN GIRI HAI!
LAGTA HAI, RAAT KI GHAM SE
AB RAHAT MILNE LAGI HAI,
AAJ FIR EK SUBHA MERE NASEEB HUYI HAI!

~ SOUDIA PARVEEN

HAAN MAIN MATLABI HI SAHI,
ISILIYE KHUDKI ZINDAGI SE ZYADA
TERA PARWA KARNE LAGI HUN!
CHAL MAIN KHUDGARZ HI SAHI,
ISILIYE TERE KHAAMOSH REHNE PAR
MANANE SABSE PEHLE MAIN HI AAJATI HUN!
KOI NAA!
MAIN DHOKEBAAZ HI SAHI,
ISILIYE GHARWALO SE JHUT BOLKAR
TUJHE WAQT DIYA KARTI HUN!
KOI BAAT NAHI,
CHAL YE BHI MAANA KI
MAIN ZIDDI HUN,
KAM SE KAM MOHABBAT KA HATH
JAKAR KE TOH RAKHTI HU!

~ SOUDIA PARVEEN

MOHABBAT KO TODHKE
WAFAYI KI MISAALEN THODI DUNGI JANAB?
MAINE BEWAFAAI BHI KISI
MAJBOORI PAR KIYA HAI!
AUR WAJAH BHI APNE MARZI SE HI NAHI DENA
CHAAHTI DUNIYA KO!
AAPKI APNI SOCH ZARUR HONGI JANAB,
PAR MERI ZUBAAN KO BHI AB KOI WAJAH DEKE
GALAT FEHMIYAN DURR NAHI KARNI!

~ SOUDIA PARVEEN

MOHABBAT KARNA BURI ADAT NAHI,
MOHABBAT PANA BURI ADAT HAI!
EK SEEMA HOTA HAI PAANE KA,
USKE BAAD BIKHADHKE DIL KO TOOTNA HI HAI
MUSHKILEN BADH JATI HAI, JEENE MAIN
KYUNKI MOHABBAT KE JAANE PAR
MAUT PYARA DIKHNE LAGTA HAI!
AKELAAPAN JIGRA DOST LAGNE LAGTA HAI
AUR KHUDKI EHSAS KO KHOON KARDENA
SAHI LAGTA HAI!

~ SOUDIA PARVEEN

HUM CHAHE JITNA BHI KOSISH KARLE
CHAAHE KITNA HI KHUDKO BADAL KYU NAH
LE!
MERA BADLAAV SIRF MUJHE HI DIKHEGA
TUMHE MEHSUS TAK NAHI HOGA AB!
KYUNKI AB MERE BADLAV
KE HAR KADAM MAIN TUMHARI
UMMEEDEIN AUR BADHNE LAGI HAI!
HUM AAJ THODA SA BADAL RE HAI,
TOH KAL KO TUM MUJHE
AUR BADALNA CHAAHOGE!

~ SOUDIA PARVEEN

TAKLIF JHELRE THE, UNHONE SAHARA LAGAYA
KHUSHIYAAN MILNE LAGI, DOSTI MAIN
APANEPAN KI MEHEK AANE LAGII!
BAATO SE LAMBI RAATEN KAT TE AAYI
PATA CHALA DOSTI M ISHQ
KI MISHRAN GHULNE LAGI HAI!
DARR DARR KE JAB UNHONE IKRAR KARNA
CHAHA,
SHABDO KA GUCCHAA ULAJHNE SI LAGI!
DOSTI PYAR M BADALKAR WO PYAR NAFRAT
MAIN NA BADAL JAAYE KAHI!
YE SOCH DIL GHABRANE PAR AAYI!
FIR HIMMAT JUTAKAR UNHONE KAHA
"MOHABBAT AGAR TOOT JAYE BHI KABHI,
YE YAARI NA CHHUTE KABHI HUMARI"
KARKE YE WADA,
NAYA MODH LAYA YE RISHTA HUMARA,
ANBAN AATA GAYA,
FIR BHI MAZBOOTI BADHTA GAYA!
DOST SE MOHABBAT
MOHABBAT SE SHAWHAR
AB WO KEHLAANE LAGA!

~ SOUDIA PARVEEN

TEEN CHAAR PURANE DOSTO K SATH,

EK RAAT MEHFIL AISI JAMI!

CHAARO TARAF SE SIRF AUR SIRF MERI HI HASI GUNJTI SUNAYI DI!

SATH HI SATH KHULE YADON KI KUCH AISI TIJORI,

BIN SAMJHE BHI MERE SATHIYO NE MILKAR MERE SATH HASA!

PICHE BUS EK HI SHAKS MERE HASNE PAR BHI NA HASA,

PUCHA GAYA JAB UNSE, "ITNI HASEEN MUSKAAN HAI FIR BHI NAZARANDAAZ KARRE HO? "

JAWAAB MAIN UNHONE KAHA,

"NAHI BUS ISKI USS HANSEE KE PICHE CHUPE DARD KO TAHE DIL SE SAMJHNE KI KOSISH MAIN LAGA HUN"

~ SOUDIA PARVEEN

CHHORA BHI NAHI JATA UNHE,
JINHE ZINDAGI MAAN LIYA HAI MAINE,
AUR ZINDAGI MAIN TOH KUCH HISSE
GHAM KI BHI PAYI JATI H,
UNN KHUSHIYO KE BHEER MAIN!

~ SOUDIA PARVEEN

JINKO MEHENDI KI KHUSHBU
SE NAFRAT HUA KARTI THII,
AAJ WO MERI HATHELI PE
LAGI MEHENDI KO CHUMTE HAI!
JINKO CHURIYO KI KHANAK SE CHIDH HOTI THI,
AAJ WO APNE PASAND SE MERE KHATIR
KANGAN KHARID LAATE HAI!
JIS INSAAN KI EK FAISLE
KO MUKAMMAL THEHRAYA JATA THAA,
AAJ WO, MERE HAR EK MANZAR PAR MERI
VICHAAR KO BHI TAWAJJUH DIYA KARTE HAI!
JINKO GHAM BHULANE KE LIYE CIGARETTE KI
SAHARA LENI PARTI THI,
AAJ MUSHKIL GHARI MAIN WO MERE SINE MAIN
SAR RAKHKE RO LIYA KARTE HAI!
INSANO KI UCHI AWAZ MAIN BAAT KARNA
JINHE SWIKAAR NAHI THA,
AAJ WO SHAKS MERE AAGE
PALKE JHUKA KE BAAT KARTE HAI!
JINKO KAAM KE LIYE IBADAT KA
WAQT NAHI MILA KARTA THAA,
AAJ WO SHAKS TAHAJJUD NI NAMAZ
MAIN MUJHE MANGA KARTA HAI!

~ SOUDIA PARVEEN

MILA KARTE THE DO SHAKS,
HAR ROZ AANGAN MAIN APNE-APNE!
DURRI GHARO KI NAHI DILO KI THI,
CHAAH ROOH KI NAHI
JISAM KI THI!
HAR ROZ KI USS SHAAM MAIN
MILAWAT DO JISMO KI HUA KARTI THII!
MOHABBAT KI PEHCHAAN ROOH SE NAHI THI
INHI DARMIYAAN,
KUCH YUN HUA KI WO DO SHAKS BICHADH KE
APNE-APNE MANZIL KI ODH BADHNE LAGE,
EK KO BEPARWAHI NE BIKHAAR DIYA!
DUSRE KO HUMRAAHI NE SAVAR DIYA!

~ SOUDIA PARVEEN

EK EK KARKE
SARI SHIKAYATEN KAGAZ MAIN
LIKHKE JALA DETI HUN,
MERE PAAS ITNA DAM KAHAN?
JO UNHI KE SAMNE NAZAR
MILAAKE UNKI HI KHAMIYA BATAUN!
EK EK KARKE
SARI GUSSA WO DEEVAR PAR
MAARKE NIKAAL DETE HAI,
UNKE PAAS UTNA HIMMAT KAHAN?
KI WO MERE UPAR HATH UTHAAYE!
EK EK KARKE
SARI CHIZEIN HUMARE RISHTE
MAIN SULAJH JAATI HAI,
ISILIYE HUMARE PYAAR MAIN ITNI PRAGYA
HAI!

~ SOUDIA PARVEEN

AKELE BETHI HUN KHIDKI KE KINARE,
JANUARY KI BAAT HAI!
USS MULAQAT KI YAAD AARI HAI HUME
NA JANE KAB WO DIN AAYEGI JAB MERE
UNGLIYO KE BICHO BICH TUMHARI UNGLI DABI
HUYI HO!
AUR NIGAHEN YUN HUMPE ATKE RAHE,
AUR TUM USS DUSRI MULAQAT MAIN NAA
JAANE KITNE KHUSH THE KI EK LAFZ BHI
BAYAN KRNA TUMHARE LIYE BOHOT KATHIN
HOGYA THAA!
KEHNE KO TOH BOHOT KUCH THAA
PAR ZUBAAN KO WO HIMMAT NHI HORA THAA!
PAR WO HUMARI DUSRI JO MULAQAT THI,
BADI HI HASEEN THII
SARD KI SHAAM THI!
BISTAR PE DONO BETHE THE,
HAATH MAIN EK CUP CHAAYE THII
AUR USS PYAAR KI IZHAR KI HI TOH INTEZAR
THII!
KHAIR,
WO BHI KYA KHUB MUKADDAR THII!
WAISE BADE YAAD AAARE HO AAJ TUM
KYUN KI BOHOT KHAAS HO TUM SABSE,
TUMHE DEKHA NHI KABSE!

~ SOUDIA PARVEEN

HAAAN BOHOT KHAAS HAI WO,
BHALE PAAS NHI HAI WO
PAR UNKI SHIRT SE MEHEKTI KHUSHBU,
AB BHI MERE JISAM SE LIPTI HUYI HAI!
HAR GHARI HAR PAL HUMSE
UNKI BATEIN TOH NAHI HOTI,
PAR UNKI ROOH KI MAUJUDGI KA EHSAAS
UNKE TAN SE BHI BADHKAR HAI!
MERI KHUSHIYO KI WAJAH NAHI,
MERI SWAYAM KHUSHI HAI WO!
MERA JAAAN NAHI,
MERA JIGAR HAI WO!

~ SOUDIA PARVEEN

USS ROZ KI EK SHAAM MAIN
JAB BARISH KI BOONDEIN GHAR KI
ANGAN MAIN AA GIREGI!
HUM AUR TUM,
USS BHAAG DAUR KI ZINDAGI
SE FIR EK BAAR PICHA CHURAKE
IKATTHE BETHENGE APNE
GHAR KE CHAUKHAT PE
KUCH TUM KEHNA KUCH HUM KAHENGE!
KUCH PURANI YAADEIN UNN NAYE
GIRTI BOOND KE TARAH FIRSE TAAZI HONGI!
TOH KAHI BICHDE MUSHKIL GHARIYO
KO UN BARISH KI GIRTI HUYI BOOND
KE TARAH MITTI MAIN MILA DENAA!
AUR HAAN,
BARSAT KI MAUSAM HO
AUR ADRAK KI CHAAYE NA HO?
BHALA YE HONE SE RAHA!
TOH FIR AAP BANAOGE NAA APNE HAATHON SE
WO CHAAYE FIR EK BAAR, HUM DONO KE LIYE?

~ SOUDIA PARVEEN

PYAALI MAIN INTEZAR,
KAR RAHI HAI HUMARI CHAAYE!
AAJ BHI RAAH DEKHTI HAI,
WO KI KAB HUM DONO
FIRSE EK AUR BAAR
SATH BETHKE KUCH YAADEIN
TAZI KARE AUR PYAALI
MAIN CHAYE JO HUMARI
INTEZAAR KARTI HAI,
USKI EK EK CHUSKEE LETE LETE
USKI TEEVRATA MAIN
TAREEFO KI PULL BAANDHE!

~ SOUDIA PARVEEN

RAAT KA WAQT HAI
HASEEN YE PAL HAI!
AIYYE MEHFIL JAMANE KI
EK AUR KOSHISH MAIN,
KUCH PURAANI YADEIN
TAAZA KIYA JAAYE,
AAJ AAPKE SATH BETHKE
FIRSE ADRAK KI CHAAYE PIYAA JAAYE!

~ SOUDIA PARVEEN

ZINDAGI TU HI BATA,
MUJHE JINE KI RAAH BATA!
UNHONE CHHOR TOH DIYA HAI
AB BATA UNKI YAADON MAIN TADPAKE,
YUN KATRA KATRA MERI LAASH BANAYEGA?
YA FIR MUJHE SHURUAAT
SE SHURU KARNE KI
HIMMAT DEGA?
YA RAAT O RAAT
KISSA KHATAM KAREGA?

~ SOUDIA PARVEEN

APNE ANDAR JHAAK KE DEKHA,
KYA KYA MANZAR JHALAKRE THE!
HAAN THODA FURSAT SE DEKHA TOH
PATA CHALA KI AAGHAT MUJHME HAI,
AUR EHSAAS UNHE DILAA RAHI THII
HAAN JAB MAINE APNE ANDAR JHAAK KE
DEKHA!
TOH PATA CHALA KI ZAKHAM MUJHME HAI,
AUR MAIN BEMATLAB KI
MARHAM UNHE LAGAYA KARTI THI!

~ SOUDIA PARVEEN

WO JISPE JAAN CHIRAKTE THE,
AAJ WO MOHABBAT HI NAHI!
TOH JAB ZINDAGI KI WO
HASEEN CHIZ HI NAHI,
TOH FIR DAR KAISA?
AB MAUT TERA DARR NAHI!

~ SOUDIA PARVEEN

~OCEAN OF QUOTES~

I write about you everytime,
whenever I open my diary!
I feel there is no more
special feeling as you,
in the entire universe!
I get words when I see you,
And my words become "Quotes"
when I admire you!
                    ~SOUDIA PARVEEN

1)Life cannot be understood until,
You ride the waves!
Float like a boat,
And swim underwater!

2)No matter which way your life leads you to,
Never go astray!
Follow the straight path,
Curved ones are always
complicated and time consuming!
Therefore both ways leads to one specific destination.

3)Life is dramatic!
So instead of being a hammy actor,
One should learn to deal
with the tantrums of it!
And strive to soothe it down
according to it's preference!

4)Just like a sea,
I am born with various waves!

5)I have loved the moon,
Ever since I left you!
I have loved the sun,
Ever since I valued my existence!
I have loved my soul,
Ever since it healed me
throughout the worst!

6)My parents are not financially rich,
But their heart is!
If you plan to buy that,
You need to strive very hard for it!

7)Freedom was gifted to me when,
I accepted myself with imperfections and Inferiorities
and decided to explore with the littles!

8)One day!
I know,
My God will ensure that he had
washed away the pain,
And painted our life with enthusiasm!
Therefore, he will come to assure that our forbearance
did not go in vain!

9)I wanna touch
Your heart deeply!
And nail it with the bloody trusts,
Let you bleed
For a while and then,
make you entirely mine!

10)Living with loved ones,
Feels like heaven inside the heart itself!

11)Relationship is bound to the theory of
"cause and effect" which states that,
To be felt good
One should make the others feel good!

12)Staring at you doesn't mean
I am in love with you,
Caring for you is definitely
what defines my love for you!

13)Love taught me,
To put forward the doubts to our beloved
Without considering the outcomes!

14)Love is a dream,
Which everyone watches!
But being loved is a dream come true,
Which a handful of people encounters!

15)Love happened when it wasn't expected,
When, the hearts were not ready to merge
It happened suddenly one night,
And was continued forever!

16)I am lost in your dreams!
But achieving mine one,
Unconsciously!

17)I am attached to the tree outside my window!
Because whenever I see it,
My mind becomes the supplier of thoughts and my
fingers starts dancing on the paper through the help of a
pen and gets indulged with the letters!

18)A woman doesn't want,
Freedom to explore!
A woman only wants,
Respect to explore without hesitation!

19)A friend is one who is available on your worst
situation,
And gives you good wishes on your success from behind
instead of asking you for a party!

20) The day I chose you,
I decided not to lose you!
Cause you are my comfort,
I got you after a lot of effort!

21) Don't use me with your hand,
Just fuse me into your land!
Perceive me with respect,
Don't perceive me as an object!

22)Heal the wound out of me,
Find out the truth behind those
Relaxed eyes!

23) You can't break me apart,
Cause I won't ever let you depart!

24)Your bitter words are pressing
my poor heart to bleed!

25) I don't want to be someone's dear,
or anyone's fear!
Because people who called me dear,
Simply broke me apart!
And the person who had a fear to loose me,
Lost me with uttermost hatred!

26)When it rains in the morning,
He gets inside my blanket slowly
And touches my neck with his warm lips!
And then, while he presses his chest against mine,
removing the locks from my face,
He whispers to my ears :
"Honey it's a moisty morning,
What if I made you a cup of hot espresso? "

27)A friendship which gets deep into an ocean
of no thresholds tends to survive the most!"

28)Your brain is a huge ocean,
Which has no threshold!
Do make the possible use of it,
to deal effectively with your surrounding!
No man is perfect but he has,
the potentiality to make things perfect!

29)The way we put concealer,
to hide our dark circles!
We put on a smile on our face,
to hide the darkest shade of our life!
So we should not misjudge
the concealer with beauty and the
smile with happiness and peace!

30)Stop putting emphasis,
on contouring your cheekbones!
When you can't afford to contour your tone while
communicating with someone!
All that matters is your behaviour,
Not beauty!

(QUOTES BY SOUDIA PARVEEN)

∼ Soudia Parveen ∼

My life is a movie which is directed by my parents.

They had never failed to come up with a conclusion to my sad chapters.

It's all because of them, everyone gets to read my penned works and it's because of their support I came up with my calibre and started exploring.

I started my journey working as a co-author and today I achieved the goal which was dreamt by my parents.

I have an ocean of goals to achieve.

This was just the beginning,

The end is too far awaiting for me.

Thankyou!
Soudia Parveen

Email: soudiaparveenpsy.0@gmail.com
Facebook: Soudia Parveen
Instagram: soudia_parveen
Website: www.yourquote.in/psychowriter
Pintrest: soudia_parveen